BOOST YOUR

VOCABULARY 1

Chris Barker

PENGUIN ENGLISH

Pearson Education Limited
Edinburgh Gate
Harlow
Essex CM20 2JE, England
and Associated Companies throughout the world.

ISBN 0 582 46877 9

First published 2001
Copyright © Chris Barker 2001

Design and typesetting by Mackerel Creative Services
Illustrations by Mark Davis
Printed in Spain by Cayfosa-Quebecor, Barcelona

Acknowledgements
The publishers make grateful acknowledgement for permission to reproduce the following copyright material:

p 15, Adam Rickitt, © Michael Melia/Retna; p 15, Kelle Destiny, © Fabrice Trombert/Retna; p 22, Rachel from S Club 7, © David Wardle/Retna; p 36, Brad Pitt, © Armando Gallo/Retna; p 48, national curriculum chart, © Crown copyright. Reproduced under the terms of HMSO Guidance Note 8; p 55, action shot of Dennis Bergkamp, © Shaun Botterill/All Sport; p 55, portrait of Dennis Bergkamp, © Gary M Prior/All Sport; p 69, catwalk, © Dorling Kindersley/Alan Williams

Published by Pearson Education Limited in association with Penguin Books Ltd, both companies being subsidiaries of Pearson plc.

For a complete list of the titles available from Penguin English please write to your local Pearson Education office or to: Marketing Department, Penguin Longman Publishing, 5 Bentinck Street, London W1M 5RN.

Contents

Introduction

Finding the right words

How many times do we want to say something in another language but we can't find the words?

Learning a language means that you start with a few words and phrases and slowly add to them. It is hardest at the beginning, because there's so much you want to say and you only have a small number of words. This is why it is important to try to increase your vocabulary as quickly as possible.

You will find that some words and phrases are more useful to you than others. You need to focus on these and try to learn them so you can use them. You don't have to learn every word or phrase.

Topics, words and phrases

In this book, we have chosen the topics which you often cover at the beginning of an English course (see the previous page for the list of contents). Under each topic, you will find important ('key') words and phrases. If you use these words and phrases frequently, you will be able to remember them better. The exercises under each topic usually start with single words, making sure you can spell them correctly, and build towards longer writing activities.

How to use *Boost Your Vocabulary 1*

You can use this book on your own, for self-study, or in a class with your teacher. It can be used in three ways:

1 **To practise and learn more vocabulary**

- Choose a topic area of interest to you.
- Read the lists of words and phrases in the topic area.
- Translate the words and phrases into your language in the spaces provided, using a good bilingual dictionary.
- Do the practice exercises. Try not to refer to the lists when you are writing.
- Check your work by looking back at the lists.
- Finally, use the Answer key to mark and correct your work.

2 **To help you with written and spoken work**

When you are working on a particular topic in class, use the lists to help you with writing or speaking.

Do the practice exercises at home to help you use the words and phrases in a variety of contexts.

3 **To revise before a test**

Test yourself on particular topics by looking at your translations and saying the English words or phrases.

Try this on your own and with a partner.

Types of exercise

There are word puzzles, quizzes, surveys and questionnaires; there are exercises which ask you to organize words into groups; and there are opportunities for continuous writing. They aim to help you remember vocabulary and use it correctly.

Symbols

Some of the exercises have symbols, to help you identify them quickly:

 spelling

 word groups

 memorization

 When you see this symbol, you should write in your notebook.

 You will also find some words and phrases in a blue box with this symbol. These focus on grammatical aspects.

Answer key

You can find the answers to the exercises and the tests in the centre of the book, in a special pull-out section.

Tests

There are tests after Units 4, 8 and 12. They revise the language of Units 1 to 4, 5 to 8 and 9 to 12. They will help you to see how well you are doing.

Self assessment and progress checks

On page 88 you will find charts which will help you to see how well you are doing and how much progress you are making.

Reference

 At the end of the book, there is a reference section. This contains a list of numbers and vocabulary to do with height and weight. It also contains a list of American English words and information on American spellings. Some basic spelling rules are also included. When you see the reference symbol you can find more information in the reference section.

1 Meeting people

Translate the words and phrases.

Saying hello and goodbye

Informal

Hi. ....

Hello. ....

Bye! ....

See you. ....

See you later. ....

See you soon. ....

See you tomorrow. ....

Formal

Good morning. ....

Good afternoon. ....

Good evening. ....

Goodnight. ....

Goodbye. ....

A: How are you? ....

B: Fine, thanks. / ....

I'm OK, thanks. ....

And you? ....

A: Mm, not too good. / ....

Mm, not great.

B: Oh, I'm sorry to hear that. ....

A: How are things? ....

B: Fine, thanks. / ....

Not bad, thanks. ....

Introducing yourself and other people

Informal

My name's (John).

....

I'm (John).

....

This is (Maria).

....

A: Nice to meet you.

....

B: Nice to meet you, too.

....

Formal

A: Let me introduce (Maria).

....

B: Pleased to meet you.

....

C: Pleased to meet you, too.

....

Welcome to (London).

....

Hi, I'm Gary.

Personal details

First name(s) ....
Surname ....
Male / Female ....
Address ....
Street ....
Town / City ....
Postcode ....
Date of birth ....
Phone number ....
Mobile phone number ....
e-mail address ....

Titles

Mr ....
Mrs ....
Miss ....
Ms ....

Male		Female	
Mr	adult men	Mrs	married women
		Miss	unmarried (single) women
		Ms	married or unmarried women

Friends

She's my best friend. ....
He's my penfriend. ....
We're good friends. ....
We're in the same class at school. ....
We're classmates. ....
We're neighbours. ....
I know him / her well. ....
I don't know him / her very well. ....
I don't get on very well with him / her. ....
We get on very / really well. ....
We don't get on very well. ....

What's your surname? ....
Could you spell that, please? ....
Could you repeat that, please? ....

You can call me Miss Tracy Bradshaw (✓) or Miss Bradshaw (✓) but not Miss Tracy (✗).

You can call me Wayne Connolly (✓) or Wayne (✓) but not Mr Wayne (✗).

You can call my Dad Mr Connolly (✓).

British	American
surname	last name
postcode	zip code
mobile phone	cellphone
penfriend	pen pal
get on	get along

1 **Complete the conversations.**

Conversation 1

A: Hello. _How_ are yo_u_?
B: Not gr__t.
A: I'm so__y __ hear that.

Conversation 2

A: Good m__ning.
   W__t's your s__name?
B: Marriott. My n__e's Ben Marriott.
A: Could you sp___ that, pl__se?
B: Yes. M A double R I O double T.
A: N_c_ to m__t you, Ben.

 2 **Complete the clues to answer the question in the crossword.**

Clues

1 We .... on really well. (3)
2 A: How are you?
   B: I'm ...., thanks. (2)
3 .... How are you? (5)
4 .... to meet you. (7)
5 My .... name is Anna. (5)
6 My .... is Smith. (7)
7 We're .... the same class. (2)
8 A: How are you?
   B: I'm ...., thanks. (4)
9 How are ....? (6)
10 It's late! I must go. ....! (9)
11 .... you tomorrow. (3)

They're very important! Who are they?

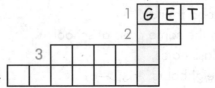

3 **Who is speaking? Write the letters in the correct pictures.**

a) Good morning, everyone.
b) Mmm, not great.
c) Hello.
d) Pleased to meet you.
e) See you later.
f) Goodnight.

4 Draw lines to link the personal details.

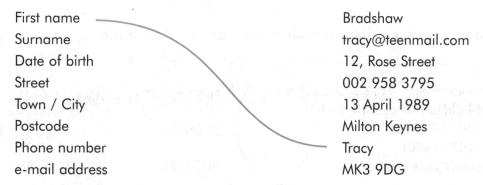

First name ——————————— Bradshaw
Surname   tracy@teenmail.com
Date of birth   12, Rose Street
Street   002 958 3795
Town / City   13 April 1989
Postcode   Milton Keynes
Phone number   Tracy
e-mail address   MK3 9DG

5 Put the words in the right order. Start with the word in the centre of each circle.

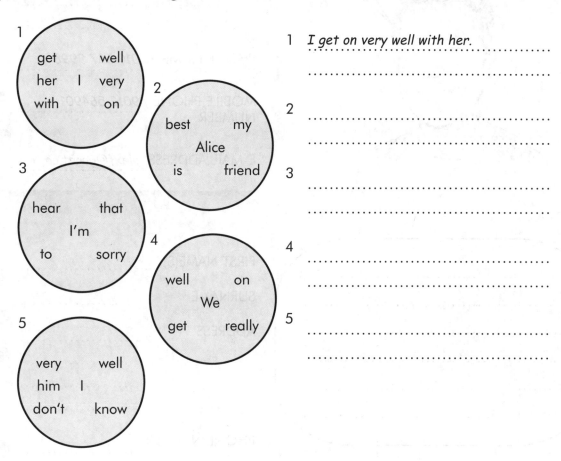

1   get   well
    her I very
    with   on

2   best   my
      Alice
    is   friend

3   hear   that
       I'm
    to   sorry

4   well   on
        We
    get   really

5   very   well
    him I
    don't   know

1   *I get on very well with her.* ....
    ....

2   ....
    ....

3   ....
    ....

4   ....
    ....

5   ....
    ....

6 Read about Tracy's best friend. Then write about your best friend.

My best friend's name is Vanessa Poole. She's thirteen.

We aren't in the same class, but we get on really well.

1

7 Read about Alex. Then complete your personal details and introduce yourself.

Hi! I'm Alex Fraser. You can contact me ...
   at 14 Clifton Road, Bath, BA4 6LH
or   on 010 587 9998
or   on 9012 564901
or   at alexf@gcnet.co.uk

FIRST NAME(S)	*Alex*
SURNAME	*Fraser*
ADDRESS	*14 Clifton Road, Bath, BA4 6LH*
PHONE NUMBER	*010 587 9998*
MOBILE PHONE NUMBER	*9012 564901*
E-MAIL ADDRESS	*alexf@gcnet.co.uk*

....
....
....
....
....
....

FIRST NAME(S)	
SURNAME	
ADDRESS	
PHONE NUMBER	
MOBILE PHONE NUMBER	
E-MAIL ADDRESS	

8a Put the missing phrases in Conversation 1 or 2.

Fine, thanks.	Hello, Mark.
I'm Rosa.	Hi.
Pleased to meet you, too.	How are you?

Conversation 1

Sarah   *Hello, Mark.* ....

Mark   Hello. ....

Sarah   ....
         Let me introduce my neighbour, Laura Green.

Laura   Hello. Pleased to meet you.

Mark   ....

Conversation 2

Kate   Hi.

Jack   ....

Kate   This is my friend.

Rosa   Hello. ....

Jack   Hi, I'm Jack.

Ouch!

Hello, Aunt Agatha. This is my friend, Wayne.

8b Which conversation is between teenagers: 1 or 2? ....

9 You are with Simon, your English penfriend. You meet one of your classmates in the street. Write the conversation.

You   *Hi.* ....

Classmate   ....

You   ....

Simon   ....

Classmate   ....

10 Write ten words and five expressions you are going to memorize.

Words		Expressions	
1	1	....	
2		....	
3	2	....	
4		....	
5	3	....	
6		....	
7	4	....	
8		....	
9	5	....	
10		....	

2 Family

Translate the words and phrases.

Male and female

boy	....	girl	....
man	....	woman	....
(plural: men)		(plural: women)	

Family members

Male		Female		Male / Female	
grandfather	....	grandmother	....	grandparent	....
grandson	....	granddaughter	....	grandchild	....
				(plural: grandchildren)	
father	....	mother	....	parent	....
Dad	....	Mum	....	guardian	....
stepfather	....	stepmother	....		
brother	....	sister	....		
stepbrother	....	stepsister	....		
halfbrother	....	halfsister	....		
husband	....	wife	....		
son	....	daughter	....		
uncle	....	aunt	....	cousin	....
nephew	....	niece	....	relation / relative	....

Life stages

baby	....
child	....
teenager	....
adult	....

Art Department

She's nice. Is she your new girlfriend?

's

Angelo = Silvia

Roberto = Sabina

Tommaso ⊥ Anna

Silvia is Tommaso's grandmother.

....

Roberto is Tommaso's father.

....

Tommaso is Anna's brother.

....

Hello. My name's Shamina. I've got a sister and a baby brother. We live with our parents in London. Our family is quite large. I've got four aunts, four uncles and seven cousins.

Hi! I'm Jonathon.

This is my sister, Tess ...

Hello!

My parents are divorced. This is my mother ...

... and these are my grandparents ...

I haven't got any aunts or uncles. Our family's quite small.

Have you got any brothers and sisters?	....
I've got a brother and a sister.	....
He's got an older sister and a younger brother.	....
I'm an only child.	....
My parents are separated.	....
My parents are divorced.	....
Our family's quite small.	....
Our family's quite large.	....

REF *See page 86 for the British / American word list.*

1 Complete the twenty family words and circle them. Look for the words horizontally (▶) and vertically (▼).

¹▼▶ ?	R	A	N	D	?	O	T	²▼ H	E	?	
³▼ U	?	C	?	E	⁴▼ B	⁵▶ C	O	?	S	?	N
⁶▶ ?	U	?	T		R	⁷▶ S	I	S	?	E	?
R	⁸▼ ?				O			?		⁹▼ W	
¹⁰▶ D	?	U	G	?	T	E	?	A		?	
I	¹¹▶ M	O	T	?	?	R	N		F		
?	¹²▼ F			E	¹³▶ ?	A	D		?		
N	A	¹⁴▶ P	?	R	E	?	T	¹⁵▼ N			
	?	¹⁶▶ G	?	A	N	D	C	?	I	?	D
	?	¹⁷▼ ?	¹⁸▶ N	E	P	?	E	?			
	?	O						?			
¹⁹▶ ?	R	A	N	D	?	A	T	H	E	?	

2 Put the words in exercise 1 into groups.

Male	Female	Male / Female
	grandmother	*guardian*

3 Who are Wayne's relations?

1 His father's mother's husband is .his grandfather.
2 His father's brother is ....
3 His mother's sister's daughter is ....
4 His sister's daughter is ....
5 His sister's son is ....

4 Choose five members of your family and write their names.

My younger brother's name is Mateo.

1 ....
2 ....
3 ....
4 ....
5 ....

5 Write details for **you** in the chart.

	Adam	**Kelle**	**you**
full name	Adam Peter Rickitt	Kellendria Trinade Roland	....
family	Mum: Jill Dad: Peter Brothers: Tim, Mark, Sam (all older)	I've got a large family: Mum, Dad and one brother; aunts, uncles and cousins.	....
boyfriend/ girlfriend	No, not at the moment.	No, not at the moment.	....
job	Actor and singer	Singer	....

6 Use the chart in exercise 5 to write about Adam, Kelle and yourself.

Adam *Hi! My full name is Adam Peter Rickitt. My mum's name is Jill and my dad's name is Peter. I've got*
....

Kelle ....
....

You ....
....

2

7a How good is your memory? You have one minute to read about Shamina and Jonathon on page 13.

Now write sentences about Shamina and Jonathon. Don't look at page 13.

Shamina

1 (brothers and sisters?)   *She's got a sister and a baby brother.*
2 (large or small family?)   ....
3 (aunts?)   ....
4 (uncles?)   ....
5 (cousins?)   ....

Jonathon

1 (sister's name?)   ....
2 (parents?)   ....
3 (grandparents?)   ....
4 (large or small family?)   ....
5 (aunts and uncles?)   ....

7b Now look at page 13 to check your answers.

8 Write the word which describes each of these life stages.

1 ....*baby*........   2 ....   3 ....   4 ....

9a Read the clues and identify the people. Write their names in the family tree.

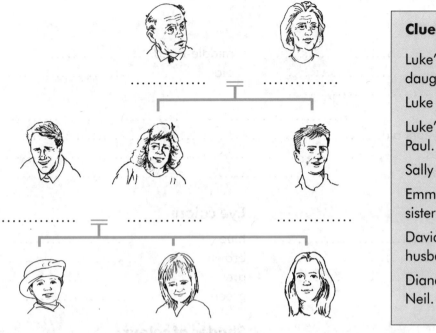

....

....

....

Clues

Luke's mum is David's daughter.

Luke is very young.

Luke's uncle is called Paul.

Sally is Paul's sister.

Emma's got a younger sister called Diana.

David and Mary are husband and wife.

Diana's father is called Neil.

9b Are you good at writing puzzles? Write some clues for a puzzle about your own family. Ask a friend to complete it.

....
....
....
....
....

10 Write ten words and five expressions you are going to memorize.

Words	Expressions
1	1 ....
2	....
3	2 ....
4	....
5	3 ....
6	....
7	4 ....
8	....
9	5 ....
10	....

3 Describing people: age and appearance

Translate the words and phrases.

Age

young	....	middle-aged	....
in her teens	....	old	....
in his twenties	....		

How old are you? ....

I'm 14. / I'm 14 years old. ....

He's in his twenties. ....

She's in her thirties. ....

Hair length

short	....
medium length	....
long	....

Eye colour

blue	....
brown	....
grey	....
green	....

Hair colour

brown	....
black	....
fair	....
blonde	....
red	....
grey	....
white	....

Shades of colour

dark	....
light	....

---

not very quite very	He's not very old.	....
	She's quite old.	....
	Her hair's very long.	....

What does he / she look like? ....

What's her hair like? ....

She's got dark brown hair. ....

What colour hair has he got? ....

He's got short, fair hair. ....

What colour eyes has she got? ....

She's got light blue eyes. ....

They're a sort of greenish brown. ....

Height

tall   ....
of medium height   ....
short   ....

Measurement of height

metre   ....
centimetre   ....
foot
(plural: feet)   ....
inch
(plural: inches)   ....

> 1 metre = 3.28 feet
> 1 centimetre = 0.39 inch
> 1 foot = 12 inches

REF See page 84 for height and weight abbreviations.

Measurement of weight

kilo   ....
stone   ....
pound   ....

Build

small   ....
big   ....
slim   ....
of medium build   ....
well-built   ....
muscular   ....

How tall is he?   ....
He's (quite) tall.   ....
He's of medium height.   ....
He's (quite) short.   ....
He's about 1 metre 75.   ....

How much do you weigh?   ....
I weigh about 50 kilos.   ....

REF See page 86 for the British / American word list.

1 Describe the age group of these people.

1 She's about 43 or 44. *She's in her forties.* ....
2 He's 52. ....
3 She's 16. ....
4 He's about 27 or 28. ....
5 She's 3. ....

2 The words in the puzzle all describe the colour and shade of hair and eyes. Complete the words.

		1▼	

2▶ **B** | | | | **D** | |

3▼ **A**

4▶ **R** | | **D**

5▶ **B** | | **A** | | **K**

6▼ **I** 7▼

8▶ **W**

9▼ 10▶ **L** | | | **T**

11▶ **G** | | **E**

3 Put the words from the puzzle in exercise 2 into the correct group. Some words can go in both groups.

Hair colour / shade	Eye colour / shade
dark..........................	dark..........................
....	....
....	....
....	....
....	....
....	....
....	....
....	....

4 How good is your maths? Use the information on page 19 to find the answers to the quiz.

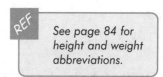

REF See page 84 for height and weight abbreviations.

QUIZ QUIZ QUIZ QUIZ QUIZ QUIZ QUIZ QUIZ QUIZ QUIZ QUIZ QUIZ QUIZ

SO YOU THINK YOU'RE GOOD AT MATHS...?

2 How tall are you?

a) in metres and centimetres? .....m....cm

b) in feet and inches? ....'.....''

3 Which is heavier?

a) 10 kg ☐

b) 20 lb ☐

1 How much do you weigh?

a) in kilos? ....kg

b) in pounds? ....lb

c) in stones and pounds? ....st.....lb

4 Which is taller?

a) 2 m ☐

b) 6' ☐

5 Use the words and phrases in the box to describe the height and build of these people.

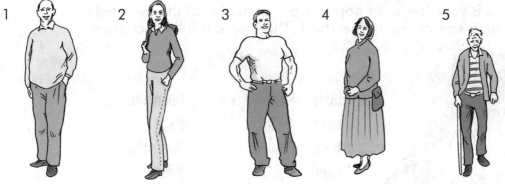

1   2   3   4   5

very	muscular	big	tall
quite	well-built	small	short
not very	of medium build	slim	of medium height

1 *He's tall and quite big.*

2 ....

3 ....

4 ....

5 ....

3

6 Write details about yourself in the chart. Then choose two members of your family or two friends and write in their details.

	you	1	2
age			
height			
weight			
build			
hair colour			
hair length			
eye colour			

7 Use the information from the chart in exercise 6 to write a description of yourself and of one of the other people.

(age and height)   *I'm fourteen and I'm 1 m 70 tall.*
(build and weight)   *I'm quite big. I weigh about sixty-seven kilos.*
(hair length and colour) *I've got long, dark brown hair*
(eye colour)   *... and brown eyes.*

My friend Tom is fifteen and he's 1 m 78 tall. He's ... He weighs ... He's got ...

8 Look at the *Star Profile* of Rachel Stevens and read about her below. Who is your favourite pop star or sports star at the moment? Write a star profile in the chart. Then write a full description.

STAR PROFILE

Full name	Rachel Stevens
Band	S Club 7
Date of birth	9th April 1978
Height	5' 3"
Hair	Light brown
Eyes	Dark brown

STAR PROFILE

Full name	....
Band / Sport	....
Date of birth	....
Height	....
Hair	....
Eyes	....

My favourite pop star at the moment is Rachel from S Club 7. Her full name is Rachel Stevens. She's in her twenties. She's 5' 3" tall. She's got light brown hair and dark brown eyes.

9 Write five quiz questions about your favourite pop star or sports star to ask a friend.

How much do you know about your favourite star? **?** **?**

1 Which pop group is .... in? /
Which sport does .... play?
a) ....?
b) ....?
c) ....?

2 What's his / her date of birth?
a) ....?
b) ....?
c) ....?

3 (height?) ....
....?
a) ....?
b) ....?
c) ....?

4 (hair?) ....
....?
a) ....?
b) ....?
c) ....?

5 (eyes?) ....
....?
a) ....?
b) ....?
c) ....?

10 Write ten words and five expressions you are going to memorize.

Words		Expressions	
1	....	1	....
2	....		....
3	....	2	....
4	....		....
5	....	3	....
6	....		....
7	....	4	....
8	....		....
9	....	5	....
10	....		....

4 House and home

Translate the words and phrases.

Description

flat	....	large	....
block (of flats)	....	small	....
house	....		

Rooms / areas

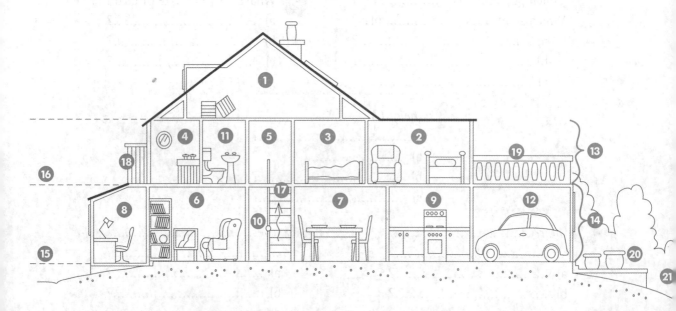

1	attic	....	12 garage	....
2	bedroom	....	13 upstairs	....
3	spare room	....	14 downstairs	....
4	bathroom	....	15 ground floor	....
5	landing	....	16 first floor	....
6	living room	....	17 stairs	....
7	dining room	....	18 balcony	....
8	study	....	19 terrace	....
9	kitchen	....	20 patio	....
10	hall	....	21 garden	....
11	toilet	....		

My room

armchair	....
bed	....
blinds	....
bookcase	....
bookshelf	....
(plural: bookshelves)	
carpet	....
ceiling	....
chair	....
chest of drawers	....
computer	....
cupboard	....
curtains	....
desk	....
door	....
duvet	....
floor	....
lamp	....
mirror	....
notice board	....
photo	....
picture	....
poster	....
radiator	....
radio	....
rug	....
shelf	....
sound system	....
table	....
telephone	....
TV	....
wall	....
wardrobe	....
washbasin	....
wastepaper bin	....
window	....

Location: prepositions

in	....
on	....
next to	....
near	....
opposite	....
between	....
in front of	....
behind	....
above	....
on top of	....
under	....
in the corner of	....
at the front of	....
in the middle of	....
at the back of	....
on the right of	....
on the left of	....

REF *See page 86 for the British / American word list.*

I live in George Street.	....
My flat is above a shop.	....
My house is near a small park.	....
It's got three bedrooms.	....
It hasn't got a garden.	....
My room is at the front of the flat.	....
What's your room like?	....
It's quite big.	....
I share my room with my sister.	....
There's a desk under the window.	....
There are some posters on the walls.	....
There are some blinds at the window.	....

4

1 Use the words in the circle to describe where you live.

house
quite   not
flat
very   small
large

I live in a house. It's very small.
....
....
....
....

2 Which parts of Wayne's house do these pictures show?

1   *the kitchen*

2   ....

3   ....

4   ....

5   ....

6   ....

7   ....

8   ....

9   ....

10   ....

3 Which of the rooms / areas in exercise 2 has your house or flat got?

My house / flat has got
....
....
....
....
....

Which other rooms / areas has it got?

It's also got
....
....
....
....
....

Which rooms / areas hasn't it got?

It hasn't got
....
....
....
....
....

4 Write the word next to the picture. Then tick (✓) the things you've got in your room. If you've got other things in your room, add them to the list.

1 ....*wastepaper bin*........ ✓

2 .... ☐

3 .... ☐

4 .... ☐

5 .... ☐

6 .... ☐

7 .... ☐

8 .... ☐

9 .... ☐

10 .... ☐

11 .... ☐

12 .... ☐

13 .... ☐

14 .... ☐

15 .... ☐

16 ....

17 ....

18 ....

19 ....

20 ....

5 Match the prepositions to the pictures.

1 near   ...*b*...
2 behind   ......
3 in   ......
4 in the corner ......
5 above   ......
6 between   ......
7 under   ......
8 on top of   ......
9 in front of   ......

a)

b)

c)

d)

e)

f)

g)

h)

i)

6 Your penfriend, William, has sent you a map and some pictures of where he lives. Complete the description.

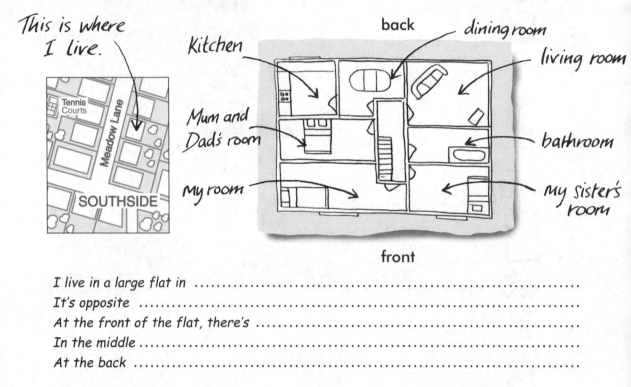

I live in a large flat in ....

It's opposite ....

At the front of the flat, there's ....

In the middle ....

At the back ....

7 Write a similar description of your house or flat to send to William.

8a William's next letter to you is about his room. Write the missing words.

1 .door............

2 ....

3 ....

4 ....

5 ....

6 ....

7 ....

8 ....

9 ....

10 ....

11 ....

12 ....

13 ....

14 ....

8b Now draw the room.

Dear .... ,

It was really good to get your letter. Thanks. Here's a description of my room. I did it on the computer. I hope you can understand it!

My room's quite large. The window is opposite the [image]¹. There are some [image]² at the window. Under the window, there's a [image]³. My [image]⁴ is on the [image], and so is my [image]⁵. There's a [image]⁶ in front of the [image] and there's a [image]⁷ between the [image] and the [image]. The [image]⁸ is next to the [image], on the right. On the left of the window, in the corner of the room, there's an [image]⁹. Between the window and the [image] there's a [image]¹⁰ with a [image]¹¹ on it. Behind the [image] there's a [image]¹². My [image]¹³ is on top of it.

That just leaves the big [image]¹⁴ where I put my clothes!

Write soon.

William

---

9 Write a description of your room for William. Use prepositions (*in, next to,* etc.) to say exactly where things are.

10 Write ten words and five expressions you are going to memorize.

Words		Expressions	
1	....	1	....
2	....		....
3	....	2	....
4	....		....
5	....	3	....
6	....		....
7	....	4	....
8	....		....
9	....	5	....
10	....		....

Test yourself 1 (Units 1 to 4)

How much can you remember?

My mark: _____
60

1 Write the words in the correct groups.

bed	cupboard	muscular	short
black	daughter	nephew	slim
blue	desk	notice board	tall
chair	green	parent	uncle
cousin	large	red	white

Family members	Height, weight and build	Colours	Furniture
1	6	11	16 .bed...........
2	7	12	17 ....
3	8	13	18 ....
4	9	14	19 ....
5	10	15	20 ....

(19 marks)

2 Match the questions to the answers.

0 How o.*ld*. are you?
1 How t.................are you?
2 How much do you w................?
3 What colour are your e................?
4 What colour is your h................?
5 What's your ph............. ....?
6 What's your p................?
7 What's your e-.............. ....?

a) 00 44 765 45 36 37
b) rocco@comtel.uk
c) light blue
d) 10 st.
e) 5'11"
f) black
h) 14
i) SL9 4PG

(7 marks)

3 Use the word in blue with one of the other words to make a sentence.

0 posters block bedroom balcony   *I've got some posters in my bedroom.*...........

1 short house hall hair   ....

2 lamp sister shelf son   ....

3 blinds window wardrobe wall   ....

4 quite tall teenager table   ....

5 small green garden grey   ....

(5 marks)

4a Complete the phrases in box A using the words in box B.

box A		box B
0 the living	*room*	drawers
1 a wastepaper	....	room
2 quite	....	of
3 in front	....	aged
4 a chest of	....	bin
5 the ground	....	old
6 a block of	....	height
7 medium	....	floor
8 a sound	....	flats
9 middle	....	system

(9 marks)

4b Use the phrases from exercise 4a to complete the description.

My grandfather is eighty-two, so he's

quite old ....[0] now. He's tall and slim.

My grandmother is fifty-two, so she's

.......................[1]. She's also quite slim.

She's of ....[2].

.......They live in ....[3] on

..................................[4]. ....

...............[5] is quite large. There's a TV and

...........................[6] in there. There's a

kitchen, a bathroom and two bedrooms. The

small bedroom is where I sleep when I stay

with them. There's a bed, and

...........................[7] the bed there's

...........................[8] for my clothes.

There's a desk with a computer on it and

...........................[9].

(9 marks)

5 Complete the dialogue.

Sam Hi, Joe.

Joe Hi, Sam. This is Gina.

Sam Hello. *Nice to meet you* ...[0]

Gina Nice to meet you, too.

Sam So, how ....[1]?

Joe Fine, ... And ....[2]?

Sam Mm, ...[3].

Joe Oh, I'm ....[4]. What's the matter?

Sam I've got problems with my girlfriend.

Joe Your girlfriend?

Sam Yes, Rebecca Sharp. You don't know her.

Joe What does ....[5]?

Sam She's quite tall and ....[6] light brown hair and green eyes. She's in Mrs Price's class.

Joe Sam ...

Sam You see, there's a girl in my class, Mandy Palmer. She's very nice. She's got long blonde ....[7] and blue eyes. We ....[8] really well.

Joe Sam ...

Gina I know Rebecca. I know her very ....[9]. In fact, she's my ....[10] friend.

Sam Oh ...

Joe ....[11] later, Sam.

(11 marks)

5 Time

Translate the words and phrases.

Days

Monday	....
Tuesday	....
Wednesday	....
Thursday	....
Friday	....
Saturday	....
Sunday	....

Years

2002	Two thousand and two
	....
1999	Nineteen ninety-nine
	....

Dates

We use ordinal numbers for dates, e.g. 1st, 2nd, 3rd, 4th. Dates can be written and spoken in different ways.

written	spoken
1st May	the first of May
May 1st	May the first

....

Time prepositions

on April 4th	....
on Monday	....
in 2002	....
in the morning	....
in the afternoon	....
in the evening	....
in (the) summer	....
at 7.30	....
at night	....
at the weekend	....

Months

January	....
February	....
March	....
April	....
May	....
June	....
July	....
August	....
September	....
October	....
November	....
December	....

Seasons

spring	....
summer	....
autumn	....
winter	....

 See page 84 for a list of ordinal numbers.

Time adverbials

tomorrow	....
yesterday	....
tomorrow morning	....
yesterday afternoon	....
last night	....
next week	....
next year	....
last week	....
last year	....

Times

one o'clock

....

two o'clock

....

five past two

....

a quarter past two

....

twenty past two

....

half past two

....

twenty-five to three

....

a quarter to three

....

ten to three

....

three o'clock

....

midday / noon ....

midnight ....

a.m. in the morning ....

p.m. in the afternoon / evening / at night ....

(Excuse me,) what time is it? ....

It's half past two. ....

What time does the film start? ....

It starts at seven o'clock. ....

What time do you get up? ....

When were you born? ....

When's your birthday? ....

It's on August 15th. ....

REF See page 86 for the British / American word list.

5

 1 Complete the days of the week.

Mo *nday* ....   Fri ....

Tue ....   Sat ....

Wed ....   Su ....

Thu ....

 2a Complete the ordinal numbers in the box.

2b Write the words from exercise 2a next to the numbers. Then write the abbreviations, as dates.

	Numbers	Words	Dates
e l e v e n t h	1	....	....
f i f t e _ n t h	2	....	....
t w e n t _ – s e _ o n d	3	....	....
f i _ s t	4	....	....
f o _ r t e _ n t h	5	....	....
t w e n t _ – f o _ r t h	11	*eleven*th	*11th* ...
s e _ _ n d	12	....	....
t h _ r d	13	....	....
t h _ r t e e n t _	14	....	....
f o _ r t _	15	....	....
t w e l _ t h	21	....	....
t w e n t _ – f _ _ s t	22	....	....
f i _ t _	23	....	....
t w e n t _ – t h _ r d	24	....	....

11

 3 Complete the months in the crossword. Then number them from 1 to 12 to show their order.

N O V E M B E R crossword grid

34   **Boost Your Vocabulary 1 Unit 5**

4 Write these dates as you would say them.

Monday, the first of January

Mon 1 JAN   Wed 4 APR   Thur 2 AUG   Sat 1 DEC

5a Complete the clues to find the mystery word.

mystery word ▼

| 1 | W | E | E | K |

| 2 | | | | |

| 3 | | | | |

| | | | | |

| 5 | | | | | |

| 6 | | | |

| 7 | | | | | | | |

1 There are seven days in it.

2 9 a.m. = nine in . . . morning

3 I can't see you this week, but I can see you . . . week.

4 7.00 = seven o' . . .

5 Between afternoon and night

6 See you . . . Saturday.

7 It's in the middle of the week.

5b Make up your own clue for the mystery word.

....

6 How do you say these times?

1   2315   *11.15 at night   a quarter past eleven at night* ....

2   0910   ....

3   1345   ....

4   0130   ....

5   1935   ....

5

7 Write the answers as you would say them.

PITT, BRAD. Actor.
(b. Dec 18th, 1963)

1 When was Brad Pitt born?

He was born on December the eighteenth, nineteen sixty-three.

2 When were you born?

....

3 At what time and in which part of the day (morning, afternoon, evening, night) were you born?

....
....

4 What's tomorrow's date?

....

5 What was yesterday's date?

....

6 What is next year?

....

8 Complete the questions and answers.

Invitation

Tracy

Come to my 18th birthday party!

Day	**Friday**
Date	**2nd Sep**
Time	**7.30 p.m. – midnight**
Place	**The Beach Club**

Bring a friend!
Love
Karen

1 Is Karen's party on Saturday? *No, it's on Friday.* ....

2 Is it on 1st September? ....

3 Is it a special birthday? Yes, ...

4 ....? At 7.30.

5 And ....? At midnight.

9a Write the names of the seasons. Then write the name of one month in each season.

Season	Month
winter	....
....	....
....	....
....	....

9b Which is your favourite season? ....

Why? ....

....

10 Write ten words and five expressions you are going to memorize.

Words		Expressions	
1	1	....
2		....
3	2	....
4		....
5	3	....
6		....
7	4	....
8		....
9	5	....
10		....

6 Life at home

Translate the words and phrases.

Before school

I get up at (7 o'clock).	....
I have a shower / bath.	....
I have a wash.	....
I brush my teeth.	....
I get dressed.	....
I listen to the radio.	....
I pack my bag.	....
I leave home at (8.30 a.m.).	....
I walk to school.	....
I cycle to school.	....
I get a lift to school.	....
I get the bus to school.	....

After school

I get home.	....
I do my homework.	....
I watch TV.	....
I take the dog for a walk.	....
I play football.	....
I play computer games.	....
I play the guitar.	....
I paint.	....
I make things.	....
I read.	....
I phone my friends.	....
I check my e-mail.	....
I send e-mails.	....
I surf the net.	....
I go skateboarding.	....
I go out with friends.	....
I go to bed.	....
I stay up late.	....

Adverbs and phrases of frequency

never	not very often	sometimes	often	usually	always

....

every day	....	a lot	....
once/twice a week	....	most evenings	....
every week	....	more than once a week	....

Jobs around the house

I tidy my room. ....

I clean the bathroom. ....

I do the vacuuming. ....

I do the washing-up. ....

I do the shopping. ....

I do odd jobs. ....

I make my bed. ....

I load the dishwasher. ....

I empty the dishwasher. ....

I put the pots away. ....

I put the rubbish out. ....

I lay the table. ....

I feed the cat. ....

I don't do anything. ....

I don't do anything.

Pets

cat ....

kitten ....

dog ....

puppy ....

parrot ....

canary ....

rabbit ....

hamster ....

guinea pig ....

goldfish ....

Meals at school and at home

I have breakfast. ....

I have a snack. ....

I have lunch. ....

I have tea. ....

I have dinner. ....

I have supper. ....

REF *See page 86 for the British / American word list.*

What time do you get up? ....

What do you do to help around the house? ....

How often do you listen to the radio? ....

What do you like doing after school? ....

I always have dinner at half past seven. ....

I usually walk to school. ....

I'm never late. ....

I like taking the dog for a walk. ....

I don't mind doing the washing-up. ....

I hate tidying my room. ....

In the morning ...

1 Complete the sentences using the verbs in the box.

brush	pack	get	have	leave

1 I *leave*.......... home.
2 I .... up.
3 I .... my teeth.
4 I .... breakfast.

5 I .... dressed.
6 I .... my bag for school.
7 I .... a wash /
    I .... a shower.

2 Write the activities in exercise 1 in the order you usually do them. Say what time you do them.

1 *I get up at 6.45.*.................
2 ....
3 ....
4 ....

5 ....
6 ....
7 ....

3a Complete sentences 1 to 8 using the words in the boxes. Add times where necessary.

breakfast	a shower	get up	dressed	I
listen to	have	the bus	usually	sometimes
always	never	a lift	the train	watch
pack	leave	get	cycle	walk

I leave home at 8.55. I never have breakfast in the kitchen.

1 ....at about .... a.m.
2 ....before breakfast.
3 ....in the kitchen.
4 ....the radio in the morning.
5 ....TV.
6 ....my school bag after breakfast.
7 ....home at .... a.m.
8 ....to school.

3b How well do you know your best friend?

Write eight similar sentences about your best friend. Then ask him / her to check if you were right.

Hannah usually gets up at about 7 a.m.
....

In the afternoon and evening ...

4 Tick the box which is correct for you.

		always	usually	often	sometimes	never
1	I watch TV.					
2	I listen to music.					
3	I play computer games.					
4	I send e-mails.					
5	I go for a long walk.					
6	I do my homework.					
7	I make dinner.					

5 Read about Zoe's afternoons and evenings. Then write about what you do after school.

When I get home from school, I always have a snack. I sometimes go out and play volleyball with my friends. I usually do my homework from about 6 o'clock to 8 o'clock. Then I have dinner. After that, I watch TV or play computer games. I often phone my friends. I never go to bed before 9.30. I always read in bed.

6 Find ten pets in the wordsearch. Then write them under the clues.

E	G	O	L	D	F	I	S	H
T	U	A	F	O	J	Z	L	A
R	I	S	I	G	K	X	A	M
Y	N	P	U	P	P	Y	B	S
I	E	D	G	H	L	C	E	T
O	A	C	A	N	A	R	Y	E
L	P	A	R	R	O	T	B	R
K	I	T	T	E	N	V	N	M
P	G	R	A	B	B	I	T	L

3   It's red, blue and yellow and it talks.
   ....

4   It's furry. It's got green eyes. The sound it makes is 'miaou'.
   ....

5   It's the same as 4, but it's very young.
   ....

6   It's light brown and it likes running in the wheel in its cage. It's about 10 cm long.
   ....

7   It's usually friendly. The sound it makes is 'woof woof'.
   ....

8   It's the same as 7, but it's very young.
   ....

9   It lives in water and it's gold and yellow.
   ....

10 It's got long ears, and it likes lettuce.
   ....

1   It's black, white and brown and it's small.
   guinea pig
   ....

2   It's small and yellow and it sings.
   ....

6

7 Circle a, b, or c. (a)

SURVEY

How often do you ...

1 help around the house?

a) most days   b) once or twice a week   c) never

2 tidy your room?

a) more than once a week   b) once a week   c) never

3 go out with friends?

a) a lot   b) two or three evenings a week   c) not very often

4 stay up after midnight?

a) most nights   b) not very often   c) never

5 play a sport?

a) two or three times a week   b) every day   c) never

6 paint, make something, play an instrument or do something creative?

a) every day   b) sometimes   c) never

 8a Write a profile of yourself using your answers to exercise 7.
Add more information or a comment to every answer.

I help around the house once or twice a week.

(Extra information) **I empty the dishwasher and put the pots away.**

I never tidy my room.

(Comment) **I hate tidying my room!**

8b Now find out what sort of person you are!

Analysis				Score	
1	a) 3	b) 2	c) 0	16 to 18	You're too good to be true! Relax!
2	a) 3	b) 2	c) 0	6 to 15	You're just right. You aren't perfect, but who wants to be perfect? You enjoy yourself and you're good with other people.
3	a) 2	b) 3	c) 1		
4	a) 0	b) 3	c) 2		
5	a) 2	b) 3	c) 0	1 to 5	Come on! You can't be untidy, lazy **and** unfriendly. Be more positive about yourself!
6	a) 3	b) 2	c) 0		

9 Write ten words and five expressions you are going to memorize.

Words	Expressions
1	1 ....
2	....
3	2 ....
4	....
5	3 ....
6	....
7	4 ....
8	....
9	5 ....
10	....

School

Translate the words and phrases.

Main school subjects in UK schools

Art	....
Art and Design	....
Citizenship	....
Design and Technology (D & T)	....
Drama	....
English Language	....
English Literature	....
Geography	....
History	....
Home Economics	....
Information Technology (IT)	....
Maths	....
Modern Languages (e.g. French, German, Spanish)	....
Music	....
Personal, Social and Health Education (PSHE)	....
Physical Education (PE)	....
Religious Studies (RS)	....
Science (Physics, Biology, Chemistry)	....

People

teacher	....
head teacher	....
deputy head	....
head of department	....
secretary	....
caretaker	....
cleaner	....
pupil	....
student	....

Exams

end-of-term exams	....
tests	....
marks	....
results	....

Non-lesson time

registration	....
assembly	....
break	....
lunchtime	....
detention	....

After-school activities and clubs

In addition to subjects on the timetable, most secondary schools in Britain offer a variety of things to do after school.

arts and crafts	....
basketball	....
chess	....
choir	....
dance	....
drama	....
film	....
football	....
homework	....
IT	....
jazz band	....
orchestra	....
photography	....
pottery	....
rugby	....
self-defence	....
swimming	....
tennis	....
volleyball	....

School rooms and places

classroom	....	canteen	....
computer room	....	hall	....
art room	....	gym	....
music room	....	changing rooms	....
laboratory	....	football pitch	....
library	....	playground	....
cafeteria	....	staff room	....

Lessons are fifty minutes long. ....

My favourite subject is English. ....

I'm good at History. ....

I'm no good at Art. ....

I'm interested in photography. ....

We have double Art on Wednesdays. ....

I'm in the football team. ....

I do pottery after school on Thursdays. ....

I go to orchestra practice on Mondays. ....

I stay late on Fridays because I do drama. ....

See pages 86 – 87 for the British / American word list.

7

abc ✓ 1 Look at Jack's timetable and answer the questions.

1 What do these abbreviations stand for?

Maths *Mathematics* ....

PE ....

RS ....

D & T ....

PSHE ....

2 Find words which describe the following times:

a) when everybody in the school is in the school hall

  assembly................................

b) when the teacher checks that all students are at school

  ....

c) when the students stop work for twenty minutes

  ....

d) when the students have a meal

  ....

3 Which language does Jack study, in addition to English?

  ....

2 Write your school timetable in English.

3 What are the differences between your timetable and Jack's?

We don't do *(school subjects)*

....

But we do *(other school subjects)*

....

We don't have *(registration, assembly)*

....

But we have

....

	JACK MOSELY				
	Mon	Tues	Wed	Thurs	Fri
8.20 am				Assembly	
	Registration				
8.40 am	Maths	PE	D & T	PE	Music
9.45 am	Science	History	Drama	Art	Science
10.45 am	Break				
11.05 am	English	Science	Maths	Geography	English
12.10 pm	French	RS	PSHE	French	D & T
1.10 pm	Lunchtime				
2.05 pm	Registration				
2.20 pm	History	Maths	English	Maths	Geography

4 Label the plan of Jack's school. The words you need are in the box, but the letters are jumbled.

tar orom	trempuco moor	sicum omor	rarbily
abrolaytor	afrecatie	fatsf moro	lalh
ymg	granyploud		

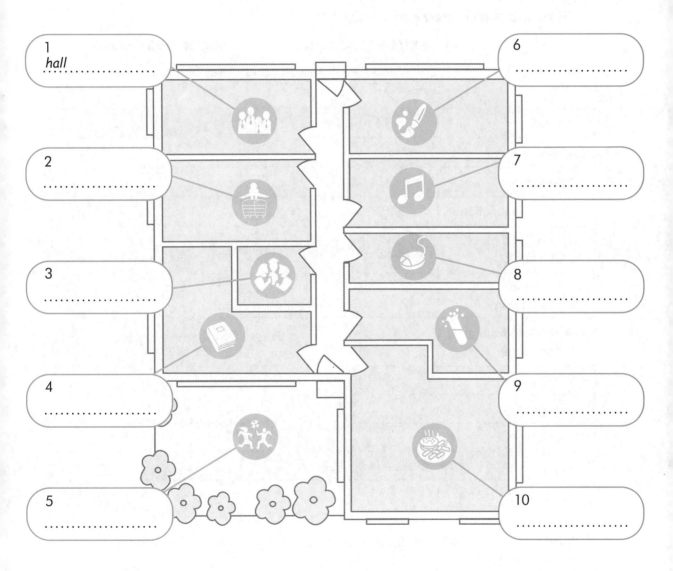

1 *hall*

2

3

4

5

6

7

8

9

10

 5 Draw a plan of part of your school and label it. Add the names of the head teacher, the deputy head, the school secretary and the head of the English department.

St Luke's School

Head teacher	*Mrs Diane Moberly*
Deputy head	*Mr James Richardson*
School secretary	*Miss Ann Bennett*
Head of English	*Ms Fiona Hartley*

6 Read the information about schools in England. Then make a chart for the subjects you study between the ages of five and sixteen. Describe the tests you have to take.

Subjects pupils have to study = ■

	PRIMARY SCHOOL		**SECONDARY SCHOOL**	
	Key Stage 1 Ages 5–7	Key Stage 2 Ages 7–11	Key Stage 3 Ages 11–14	Key Stage 4 Ages 14–16
English	■	■	■	■
Mathematics	■	■	■	■
Science	■	■	■	■
Physical education	■	■	■	■
Design and technology	■	■	■	■
Information technology	■	■	■	■
A modern foreign language			■	■
History	■	■	■	
Geography	■	■	■	
Music	■	■	■	
Art	■	■	■	
Citizenship			■	■

Schools organize their own timetables, and can decide what other subjects to teach their pupils.

National tests and examinations pupils have to take

There are national tests for 7-, 11- and 14-year-olds in English and Mathematics. Pupils aged 11 and 14 also have tests in Science. Most 16-year-olds take the GCSE (General Certificate of Secondary Education) exam in several subjects (usually between five and ten).

7 Put these after-school activities and clubs into groups. Tick (✓) the ones you do and double tick (✓✓) the ones you'd like to do.

arts and crafts
basketball
chess club
choir
computer club
football
French film club
jazz band
orchestra
photography club
pottery
salsa club
Spanish club
swimming
tennis
volleyball

sports and games

basketball...........
....
....
....
....
....

music and dance

choir
....
....
....
....

CLUBS AND ACTIVITIES

practical and creative skills

arts and crafts
....
....
....
....

languages

French film club...
....

8 Complete Joanne's account of her school.

I go to Chadworth School. It's a s e c o n d a r y [1] school with 950 students aged eleven to eighteen. It's a mixed school, but boys and girls have separate l _ _ _ _ _ _ [2]. The teachers say we get better exam r _ _ _ _ _ _ [3] that way.

My favourite subjects are French and Spanish. I love l _ _ _ _ _ _ _ _ [4]. And I'm really interested in the cinema, so I go to f _ _ _ [5] club every Thursday.

I'm from a large family and we live in a small flat. It's difficult to concentrate on your work there, so I sometimes go to h _ _ _ _ _ _ _ [6] club after school. I'm not very sporty, but we've got a great pool at the school so I go to s _ _ _ _ _ _ _ [7] club on Saturdays.

9 Write ten words and five expressions you are going to memorize.

Words		Expressions	
1	....	1	....
2	....		....
3	....	2	....
4	....		....
5	....	3	....
6	....		....
7	....	4	....
8	....		....
9	....	5	....
10	....		....

8 Sport

Translate the words and phrases.

Sport/Activity		Person	
Play	*I play football*		
football	....	footballer	....
American football	....	footballer	....
badminton	....	badminton player	....
baseball	....	baseball player	....
basketball	....	basketball player	....
cricket	....	cricketer	....
golf	....	golfer	....
field hockey	....	hockey player	....
ice hockey	....	hockey player	....
rugby	....	rugby player	....
squash	....	squash player	....
table tennis (ping pong)	....	table tennis player	....
tennis	....	tennis player	....
Do	*I do gymnastics*		
gymnastics	....	gymnast	....
athletics	....	athlete	....
aerobics	....	'I do aerobics'	....
yoga	....	'I do yoga'	....
weightlifting	....	weightlifter	....
Go	*I go canoeing*		
canoeing	....	canoeist	....
rock climbing	....	rock climber	....
motor racing	....	racing driver	....
Go	*I go riding or I ride*		
riding	....	rider	....
cycling	....	cyclist	....
running	....	runner	....
sailing	....	sailor	....

Sport/Activity

(Go)

skiing	....
surfing	....
swimming	....
windsurfing	....
ice skating	....
fishing	....

I box

boxing	....
diving	....
scuba diving	....
rowing	....

Person

skier	....
surfer	....
swimmer	....
windsurfer	....
ice skater	....
'I fish' / 'I go fishing'	....

boxer	....
diver	....
scuba diver	....
rower	....

Sports events

game	....
match	....
competition	....
championship	....
tournament	....
the Olympics	....
the World Cup	....
the Cup Final	....

Winning and losing

gold medal	....
silver medal	....
bronze medal	....
cup	....
to come first / last	....
to be the winner / loser	....
to be the runner-up	....

I'm quite a good swimmer.
....

I'm quite sporty.
....

I'm not very fit.
....

I'm not very good at diving.
....

I can swim but I can't dive.
....

I'm not very keen on sport.
....

I like watching motor racing.
....

I'd like to go skiing.
....

I'd like to try windsurfing.
....

Bring your swimming gear.
....

Which football team do you support?
....

I'm an Arsenal fan.
....

They lost the match by two goals to one.
....

She won a gold medal.
....

 For sports clothes, see Fashion, page 64. See page 87 for the British / American word list.

1 **Complete the words.**

c a n o e i n g	w _ n _ su _ fing	sq _ as _
fo _ _ ball	Ameri _ _ n _ o _ _ ball	cri _ ket
s _ r _ ing	s _ ub _ d _ v _ ng	sa _ ling
t _ n _ is	b _ s _ ball	r _ g b _
swim _ ing	bas _ _ tball	ta _ le ten _ is

2 **Put the words in exercise 1 into groups.**

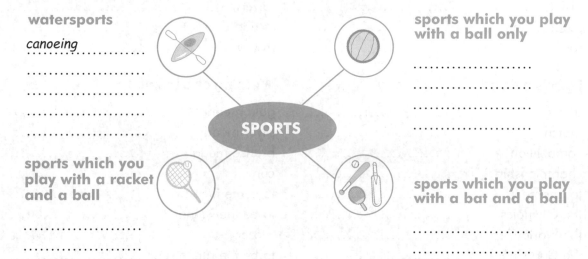

watersports

canoeing

....

....

....

....

sports which you play with a ball only

....

....

....

....

SPORTS

sports which you play with a racket and a ball

....

....

sports which you play with a bat and a ball

....

....

3 **Name the sports and say who does them.**

1 2 3 4 5 6 7 8 9 10

	Sport	Person		Sport	Person
1	athletics	athlete	6	....	....
2	....	....	7	....	....
3	....	....	8	....	....
4	....	....	9	....	....
5	....	....	10	....	....

4 Answer the questions.

How sporty are you?

Answer these questions to find out.

1 Can you swim?

......•.................

2 Can you dive?

....

3 Can you run ten kilometres?

....

4 Can you ice skate?

....

5 Can you name three people who are well known in three sports?

....

....

6 Which sports do you like doing?

....

....

7 Which sports do you watch on TV?

....

....

8 Which sports do you think are really boring?

....

....

9 Which sports would you like to try?

....

....

10 Which sports do people in your family do?

....

....

5a Read the interviews. Then cover them and answer the questions.

Journalist	Hannah, you're quite sporty, aren't you?
Hannah	Yes, I suppose I am. I go swimming twice a week. And I do a dance class when I've got time.
Journalist	Do you play any ball games?
Hannah	Yes, I play football every Saturday. We won last Saturday's game 3-0!
Journalist	Well done! Are there any sports you'd like to try?
Hannah	Yes, I'd like to try windsurfing.
Journalist	Are you sporty, David?
David	Well, not really. I quite enjoy swimming, but that's about all.
Journalist	Do you like watching sport?
David	Yes, I like watching motor racing on TV. And I went to Monza in Northern Italy last year. It was really exciting.
Journalist	Are there any sports you'd like to try?
David	I'd like to try scuba diving.

1 Are Hannah and David both good at sports? ....
2 What does David think of motor racing? ....
3 What did Hannah do last Saturday? ....
4 Which watersports would Hannah and David like to try? ....
....

 5b Now write an interview between the journalist and you.

6 Answer the clues to complete the sports crossword.

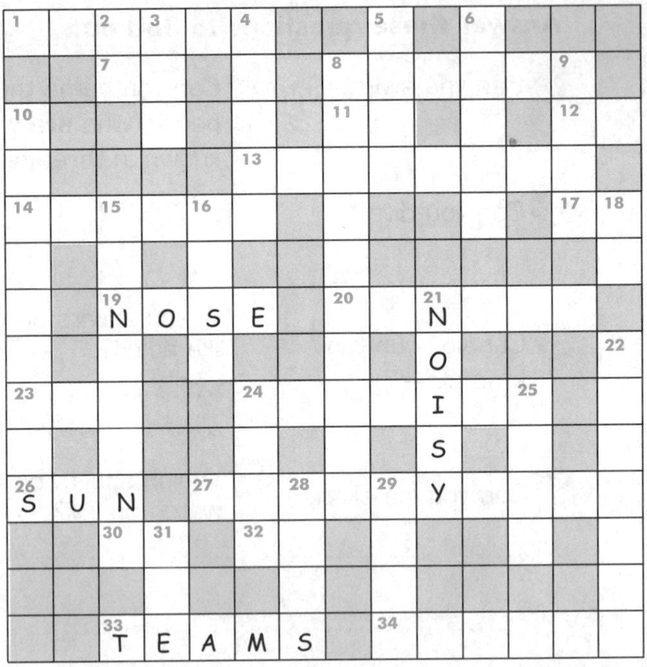

Across

1 Who's your favourite tennis. . .? (6)
7 I'd like . . . try bungee jumping (2)
8 It's a sport in which people fight each other. (6)
11 She's . . . excellent athlete. (2)
12 I usually go swimming . . . Tuesdays. (2)
13 You play it with a bat like this and a ball like this. (8) 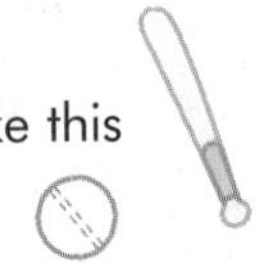
14 There are two types of this sport. One type is played on ice. (6)
17 Do you . . . gymnastics at school? (2)
19 I don't like diving. The water gets up my . . .! (4)
20 Another name for ping pong: table . . . (6)
23 and 24 You do this sport on frozen water. You don't need a stick. (3, 7)
26 Surfing is more fun when the . . . is shining. (3)
27 You can play this ball game on the beach. (10) 
30 Let's . . .swimming! (2)
32 Come with us. . . . 're going fishing. (2)
33 Manchester United and Chelsea are famous football . . . (5)
34 You need a horse for this sport. (6)

Down

2 Which sports are you good . . .? (2)
3 Paul, can . . . dive? (3)
4 You play it with a ball like this. (5) 
5 Sorry, William isn't here. He's . . . fishing. (4)
6 I've got tickets for the Cup . . . (5)

8 You score baskets in this game. (10)
9 The top Olympic medal. (4)
10 Running, high jump, long jump, etc. (9)
15 You need one of these for this sport. (8) 
16 Do you think rock climbing is difficult or . . .? (4)
18 I'm not very keen . . . sport. (2)
21 Fishing is a quiet activity; motor racing is . . . (5)
22 You need a boat for this sport. (7)
24 It's white, and you need it for skiing. (4)
25 I can't go swimming. I haven't got my . . . (= swimming costume, towel, goggles) (4)
28 To swim well, you need strong arms and . . . (4)
29 Do you . . . go cycling at weekends? (4)
31 We scored three goals and the other team scored two. We won by . . . goal. (3)

Crossword grid answers shown:
19 across: N O S E
21 down: N O I S Y
26 across: S U N
33 across: T E A M S

7 Read this profile of Dennis Bergkamp. Then write a profile of a sports star.

Dennis Bergkamp

SPORTS STAR
OF THE WEEK

Name	Dennis Bergkamp
Nickname	'The non-flying Dutchman'
Sport	Football
Team	Arsenal
Did you know?	He speaks four languages.
	He won't fly anywhere. That's why his nickname is 'The non-flying Dutchman'.
Recent achievements	He played in the Dutch team in Euro 2000. They reached the semi-finals.

Can I just ask … is this your first time on a horse?

8 Write ten words and five expressions you are going to memorize.

Words	Expressions
1	1 ....
2	....
3	2 ....
4	....
5	3 ....
6	....
7	4 ....
8	....
9	5 ....
10	....

Test yourself 2 (Units 5 to 8)

How much can you remember?

1 Complete the expressions with *in*, *on* or *at*.

0 ...*in*... the morning   4 ...... Tuesday
1 ...... night   5 2001
2 ...... the weekend   6 ...... July 4th
3 ...... the summer

                              (6 marks)

2 In the correct order, write ...

1 the parts of the day   *morning*.....................................
2 the seasons   *spring*...
3 the dates of the first four days of a month *first*...................

                              (9 marks)

3 Write sentences for these pictures describing Amy's day.

0

She gets up at seven o'clock.
....

3

....

1

....

4

....

2

....

5

....

                              (5 marks)

4 Complete these sentences about life at home. Think of phrases to do with:

- • what you do before school
- • what you do after school
- • meals
- • jobs around the house

0 I usually have *a shower before breakfast.* ....

1 I have ....

2 I get ....

3 I go ....

4 I sometimes do ....

5 I often make ....

(10 marks: 2 marks for each sentence)

5 Write the names of three ...

1 school subjects: *Geography* ....

2 school rooms or areas: *laboratory* ....

3 people who work at school: *caretaker* ....

4 non-lesson times: *detention* ....

5 after-school activities: *pottery* ....

6 meals: *supper* ....

7 pets: *canary* ....

8 sports people play: *golf* ....

9 activities people do: *yoga* ....

10 people who do sports: *golfer* ....

(30 marks)

But you said "Let's play football!"

9 Free time

Translate the words and phrases.

Activities

go shopping	....
go rollerblading	....
go skateboarding	....
go clubbing	....
go to a football match	....
go to a friend's house	....
go to a disco	....
go to a concert	....
go to a party	....
go to the beach	....
go to the cinema	....
go to the theatre	....
go to the park	....
go to the (swimming)	....
pool	....
go to see a film	....
go to see a band	....
go out with friends	....
go out with a boyfriend	....
/ girlfriend	....
go out for a meal	....
go out dancing	....
play on the computer	....
play computer games	....
play in the street	....
play the piano	....
have a party	....
listen to music	....
read magazines	....
read a book	....
collect stamps / coins /	....
phone cards	....
relax	....
stay over at a friend's	....
house	....
surf the net	....
watch TV	....
watch a video	....

REF *See Sport on pages 50 – 51 for more activities.*

Talking about past activities

What did you do last weekend?

....

....

I went to the cinema with my boyfriend.

....

....

We saw Star Wars.

....

I played basketball with my friends.

....

....

I went to a football match.

....

....

We had a party. It was great.

....

....

I didn't do anything.

....

I stayed at home and watched TV.

....

....

Music

classical music	....
dance music	....
folk	....
heavy metal	....
hip hop	....
jazz	....
Latin music	....
pop music	....
rap	....
reggae	....
R 'n' B	....
(rhythm and blues)	....
rock	....
salsa	....
techno	....

Musical instruments

cello	....
clarinet	....
double bass	....
drums	....
flute	....
guitar	....
keyboards	....
organ	....
piano	....
recorder	....
saxophone	....
tambourine	....
trumpet	....
violin	....

What kind of music do you like?   ....

It's got a good beat.   ....

It's good to dance to.   ....

It makes you feel good.   ....

It's very dramatic.   ....

It's relaxing.   ....

It's good to listen to when you're working.   ....

I don't know why I like their new single. I
  just do!   ....
         ....

What do you do in your free time?   ....

I sometimes go to the cinema.   ....

I enjoy going to the cinema.   ....

I don't do much after school.   ....

I love the internet and e-mail.   ....

I go to drama school on Saturdays.   ....

Yes, darling, of course you can go to the cinema this evening.

REF

See page 38 for adverbs and phrases of frequency. See page 87 for the British / American word list.

9

1 What do you do in your free time? Write sentences using the words and phrases below.

I

often
sometimes
never

go
go to
listen to
play   go out
read   surf
watch

shopping
soaps on TV
concerts   the net
a football match
the guitar (piano, etc.)   concerts
dancing   a friend's house
parties   for a meal
magazines   music
with friends

1 *I sometimes go to concerts.*..................
2 ....
3 ....
4 ....
5 ....
6 ....
7 ....
8 ....
9 ....
10 ....

2 Complete the sentences. Remember to use *like + -ing.*

In my free time I really like ...

1 ....
2 ....
3 ....

In my free time I really like listening to music. I don't like going shopping.

In my free time I quite like ...

1 ....
2 ....
3 ....

In my free time I don't like ...

1 ....
2 ....
3 ....

3 You have just received a letter from a new penfriend. Complete the letter with Jess's free time activities.

Hi!

You asked me what I do in my free time. Well, I thought I'd send you a puzzle, to see if you can work it out!

During the week, I sometimes .....*go to the pool*..... ¹ after school.

If I haven't got a lot of homework, I .... ²,

.... ³ or .... ⁴.

Some friends and I are in a band. I .... ⁵ I really enjoy

.... ⁶.

Of course, if I'm tired, I just .... ⁷ or

.... ⁸. I really like .... ⁹.

On Saturdays, I .... ¹⁰ with friends in the

morning and then in the afternoon we sometimes .... ¹¹.

Oh, and I almost forgot! I .... ¹² So if you've got

any old ones, please send them to me! And tell me what you do in your free time.

Bye for now

Jess

4 Write a reply to Jess.

5 Write the names of the instruments in groups to help you remember them.

piano ....

organ ....

....

....

....

....

....

....

MUSICAL INSTRUMENTS

....

....

....

....

....

....

....

....

6 Write sentences about Julie and Andy's week using the past tense verbs in the box.

played	watched	had	went	saw

Monday

Toy Story 2

SCREEN 6   ROW R   SEAT 15

On Monday, they went to the cinema.

Tuesday

TODAY'S TV

MATCH OF THE DAY
ENGLAND vs ROMANIA
7pm BBC1

....

Wednesday

HAMLET
Dress Circle
Doors open 7.00pm
Performance starts 7.45pm

....

Thursday

Andy,
Here's the shopping list.
Sorry, I can't help, I'm
playing volleyball.
Love Julie

bread, milk,
coffee, eggs,
tomatoes, rice

....
....

Friday

Julie and Andy
invite you to a party
on
Saturday 15th August
at
7.30pm

....

7 Write five sentences about things you did last week. Say when you did them. The verbs in exercise 6 may help you.

A week ago, I went to a party.

Last night, I watched a really good programme on TV.

8a Who are your top three composers / musicians / bands of all time?

Composer / Musician / Band	Type of music
1	....
2	....
3	....

8b What's your favourite single at the moment? Say why you like it.

My favourite single at the moment is ....

I like it because ....

9 Read about Tamara. Then write a similar profile of yourself.

On Saturdays, I get up at about ten o'clock. I go shopping with my mum. I see my friends in the afternoon and in the evening I surf the net or just relax. I listen to a lot of Latin music. I love salsa. I sometimes go to the cinema or go ice skating with my friends.

There isn't much to do where I live, because it's very quiet, not in the city centre. I'd like to live in London. I'd like to be right in the middle of things, with lots of things to do.

10 Write ten words and five expressions you are going to memorize.

Words	Expressions
1	1 ....
2	....
3	2 ....
4	....
5	3 ....
6	....
7	4 ....
8	....
9	5 ....
10	....

10 Fashion

Translate the words and phrases.

Colours

black	....	purple	....
blue	....	red	....
brown	....	silver	....
cream	....	white	....
gold	....	yellow	....
green	....		
grey	....		

Shades

orange	....
pink	....

light (blue) ....
dark (blue) ....

Clothes and footwear

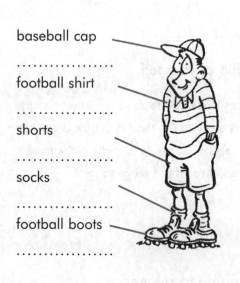

baseball cap
....

football shirt
....

shorts
....

socks
....

football boots
....

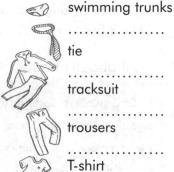

fleece
....

gloves
....

jacket
....

jeans
....

pants
....

scarf
....

sweatshirt
....

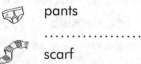 

swimming trunks
....

tie
....

tracksuit
....

trousers
....

T-shirt
....

vest
....

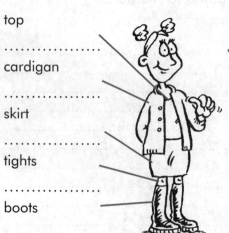

top
....

cardigan
....

skirt
....

tights
....

boots
....

 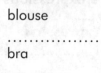 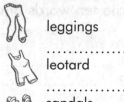

blouse
....

bra
....

coat
....

dress
....

hat
....

jumper
....

knickers
....

  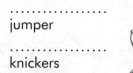

leggings
....

leotard
....

sandals
....

shirt
....

shoes
....

swimming costume
....

trainers
....

Parts of clothes

 sleeve ....

 button ....

 pocket ....

 collar ....

 zip ....

Style

long	....	cropped	....
short	....	long-sleeved	....
big	....	short-sleeved	....
small	....	sleeveless	....
baggy	....	knee-length	....
tight	....	ankle-length	....

(*Clothes*) What size are you? ....

(*Shoes*) What size do you take? ....

Do you like this one? ....

Do you like these? ....

Can I try it on? ....

Have you got it in another colour? ....

How much is it? ....

Does it suit me? ....

It suits you. ....

It looks good on you. ....

You look nice. ....

It's a pretty dress. ....

It's too small. ....

It doesn't fit. ....

They're really fashionable at the moment. ....

They're really in at the moment. ....

I like that jacket. It's cool. ....

What are you going to wear? ....

I'm going to wear ... .

What did you wear? ....

I wore ... .

 See page 87 for the British / American word list.

abc ✓ **1** Complete the colours. Then think of an object to associate them with.

1 blu _e_   *my blue jeans* ....   7 oran__ e   ....
2 sil _v_ er *a silver ring* ....   8 pi__k   ....
3 blac__   ....   9 pu__ple   ....
4 go__d   ....   10 r__d   ....
5 gre__n   ....   11 w__ite   ....
6 gre__   ....   12 yello__   ....

2 There are eighteen items of clothing or footwear in the wordsearch. Some are more than one word. Circle them.

B	A	S	E	B	A	L	L	C	A	P	S	H	V	J	L	M
L	E	G	G	I	N	G	S	B	R	A	W	I	E	U	E	O
O	J	E	A	N	S	K	N	I	C	K	E	R	S	M	O	S
U	H	A	T	P	C	A	R	D	I	G	A	N	T	P	T	K
S	W	I	M	M	I	N	G	C	O	S	T	U	M	E	A	I
E	B	O	O	T	S	T	R	O	U	S	E	R	S	R	R	R
J	A	C	K	E	T	L	T-S	H	I	R	T	B	C	D	T

3 Use the adjectives in the box to describe these articles of clothing.

baggy	knee-length	sleeveless	short
long	long-sleeved	short–sleeved	

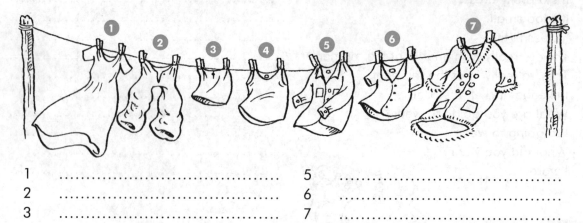

1 ....   5 ....
2 ....   6 ....
3 ....   7 ....
4 ....

4 Group all the words in the wordsearch on page 66 under the headings in the chart and tick (✓) the correct columns. Use each word once only.

		men	women	underwear	sports clothing	worn on the head
clothes worn on the whole body						
	leotard		✓		✓	
clothes worn on the top half of the body						
	baseball cap	✓	✓		✓	✓
clothes worn on the bottom half of the body and footwear						
	skirt		✓			

5 Write the letters in the correct speech bubbles.

a *I'd like to try this dress on ...*
b Do you like these boots?
c How do I look, boys?
d How is it?
e And some purple boots.
f I'll take ...
g ... it really suits you.
h They look fantastic.
i What size are you?

6 Name two items of clothing which have the following parts. Try to put something different each time.

1 collar *shirt* .... *blouse* ....
2 sleeve ....
3 pocket ....
4 zip ....
5 button ....

7 What are Tracy and Wayne going to wear tonight? You decide. Be as imaginative as you like!

Tracy's going to wear...
....
....
....

Wayne's going to wear...
....
....
....

8 Write sentences to answer the fashion questionnaire.

Fashion Statement

1 What are you wearing now?

2 What do you like wearing?

3 What looks cool at the moment for boys? / for girls?

4 Which colours are fashionable at the moment?

5 What would you wear to a party?

9 Write ten words and five expressions you are going to memorize.

Words	Expressions
1	1 ....
2	....
3	2 ....
4	....
5	3 ....
6	....
7	4 ....
8	....
9	5 ....
10	....

11 Food and drink

Basic food

bread ....

butter ....

cereal ....

cheese ....

eggs ....

fish ....

fruit ....

margarine ....

meat ....

nuts ....

oil ....

pasta ....

rice ....

salt and pepper ....

sugar ....

vegetables ....

vinegar ....

yoghurt ....

Fruit

apple ....

apricot ....

banana ....

cherry ....

coconut ....

grape ....

grapefruit ....

kiwi ....

lemon ....

melon ....

orange ....

peach ....

pear ....

pineapple ....

plum ....

raspberry ....

strawberry ....

Drinks

mineral water (still, ...

  sparkling) ....

fruit juice (orange ....

  juice, apple juice) ....

lemonade ....

milk ....

milkshake ....

cola ....

beer ....

wine (white wine, ...

  red wine) ....

tea ....

coffee ....

hot chocolate ....

Sandwiches? We've got cheese, egg, ham, beef, tomato and cucumber.

Sounds good. I'll have one of those.

Vegetables

aubergine	....	lettuce	....
bean	....	mushroom	....
broccoli*	....	onion	....
cabbage	....	pea	....
carrot	....	pepper	....
cauliflower	....	(red pepper, green pepper)	
celery*	....	potato	....
courgette	....	(plural: potatoes)	
cucumber	....	spinach*	....
garlic*	....	tomato	....
		(plural: tomatoes)	

Meat

bacon	....
beef	....
chicken	....
duck	....
ham	....
lamb	....
pork	....
sausage	....
turkey	....

Aubergines, peppers and tomatoes are types of fruit, but we use them in vegetable dishes.

* These nouns do not have plurals.

REF See page 87 for the British / American word list.

Prepared food

biscuit	....	kebab	....
cake	....	omelette	....
chips	....	pancake	....
crisps	....	pizza	....
curry	....	salad	....
hamburger	....	sandwich	....
hot dog	....	soup	....
ice cream	....	toast	....
jam	....	waffle	....

I'm thirsty. ....

I could do with a drink. ....

Can I have an orange juice, please? ....

I'll have a lemonade. ....

I'm hungry. ....

I could do with something to eat. ....

What would you like? ....

Do you fancy a sandwich? ....

What's your favourite dish? ....

What are the ingredients? ....

What's for pudding? ....

1 Solve the crossword.

Across ▶

1 (4)

4 (4)

6 (8)

7 (4)

8 A late meal. (6)

11 (3)

12 (5)

14 (5)

15 An afternoon meal. Also a drink. (3)

16 (6)

17 . . . cream. (3)

Down ▼

2 I'm hungry. Is there anything to . . . ? (3)

3 Have . . . fruit. (4)

4 (6)

5 (4)

7 (6)

8 (8)

9 (8)

10 (7)

13 (4)

1	**2**		**3**			**4** B	E	E	**5** F	
		6								
					7					
8		**9**								
									10	
11 N	U	T		**12**		**13**				
14										
						15				
16										
						17				

2 Tick (✔) A or B in this quiz.

Quick quiz

Which do you prefer ...

1	with a meal?	**A** cola	*or*	**B** water
2	for pudding?	**A** pancakes	*or*	**B** fruit
3	with fish?	**A** chips	*or*	**B** a salad
4	for a snack?	**A** a hot dog	*or*	**B** an apple
5	before bed?	**A** coffee	*or*	**B** milk
6	for breakfast?	**A** bacon and eggs	*or*	**B** some yoghurt
7	for lunch?	**A** sausages	*or*	**B** fish
8	after school?	**A** a kebab	*or*	**B** a sandwich
9	at the cinema?	**A** crisps	*or*	**B** nuts
10	to give you energy?	**A** sugar	*or*	**B** a banana

Analysis More As than Bs: Try to eat more food from the B list. More Bs than As: Well done! You eat well.

3 Label the ingredients for these dishes.

moussaka

1 .... lamb ....

2 ....

3 ....

4 ....

5 ....

6 ....

7 ....

8 ....

salad

1 ....

2 ....

3 ....

4 ....

5 ....

4 What's your favourite dish called? What are the ingredients?

Name of dish: ....

Ingredients:
....
....
....
....
....
....
....
....

Name of dish: Fish and chips
Ingredients: Fish
Chips

5 Answer the questions from the *Food Facts* survey in *T2 Magazine*.

1 Look at the top five breakfasts according to a survey in *T2 Magazine*. Which do you think was the most popular? Put them in order using numbers 1 to 5 (number 1 = the most popular).

FOOD FACTS

Survey: the top five breakfasts

.... bacon and eggs
.... cereal
.... fruit
.... toast / croissants
.... waffles

2 *T2 Magazine* asked British 7- to 16-year-olds about their favourite food. Put these four kinds of food (taken from the ten favourites) in order using numbers 1 to 4 (number 1 = the most popular).

FOOD FACTS

Survey: the top ten favourite kinds of food in Britain

.... pasta
.... Chinese food
.... curry
.... pizza

6 If you asked 7- to 16-year-olds in your country for their top ten favourite dishes, what do you think the answers would be?

Top ten favourite dishes in   ....

1 ....   6 ....
2 ....   7 ....
3 ....   8 ....
4 ....   9 ....
5 ....   10 ....

7 Write your answers to the questionnaire.

Meals and meal times	Nicholas	You
breakfast What time do you have breakfast? What do you have for breakfast?	I usually have breakfast at 8 o'clock. I have cereal, a yoghurt and apple juice.	
lunch What time do you have lunch? Where do you have lunch? What do you have for lunch?	12.30 p.m. I have lunch at school. I have sandwiches, crisps, some fruit and a drink.	
tea / snack What time do you have a snack? What do you eat?	4.30 p.m. When I get home from school, I have a biscuit, or some bread.	
dinner What time do you have dinner? What do you have for dinner?	We have dinner at about 6 o'clock. I sometimes have pasta with chicken or a pizza.	
favourites What are your favourite dishes?	My favourite breakfast is scrambled eggs on toast. My favourite lunch is a cheese sandwich and a yoghurt. My favourite dinner is spaghetti bolognese.	
dislikes What food don't you like?	I hate cabbage and spinach.	

 8 Write ten words and five expressions you are going to memorize.

Words	Expressions
1	1 ....
2	....
3	2 ....
4	....
5	3 ....
6	....
7	4 ....
8	....
9	5 ....
10	....

12 Countries, nationalities and languages

Translate the words and phrases.

> This unit only includes a selection of countries. Use an atlas and a dictionary to find some more countries and nationalities in each section.

Some countries and nationalities

Europe

Belgium / Belgian	....	Italy / Italian	....
Denmark / Danish	....	Norway / Norwegian	....
England / English	....	Poland / Polish	....
France / French	....	Portugal / Portuguese	....
Germany / German	....	Scotland / Scottish	....
Greece / Greek	....	Spain / Spanish	....
Holland / Dutch	....	Sweden / Swedish	....
Hungary / Hungarian	....	Switzerland / Swiss	....
Ireland / Irish	....	Wales / Welsh	....

The United Kingdom (The UK)	....	The Netherlands	....
		Scandinavia	....

Europe / Asia

Russia / Russian	....	Turkey / Turkish	....

Middle East and Asia

China / Chinese	....	Malaysia / Malaysian	....
India / Indian	....	Pakistan / Pakistani	....
Indonesia / Indonesian	....	Saudi Arabia / Saudi Arabian	....
Iran / Iranian	....	Thailand / Thai	....
Iraq / Iraqi	....		
Israel / Israeli	....		
Japan / Japanese	....		

North America

Canada / Canadian	....
The United States of America (The USA) / American	....

Central America

Mexico / Mexican	....
Nicaragua / Nicaraguan	....

South America

Argentina / Argentinian .... Peru / Peruvian ....

Bolivia / Bolivian .... Uruguay / Uruguayan ....

Brazil / Brazilian ....

Chile / Chilean .... Venezuela / Venezuelan ....

Columbia / Columbian ....

Africa

Algeria / Algerian .... Nigeria / Nigerian ....

Egypt / Egyptian .... South Africa / South African ....

Ethiopia / Ethiopian ....

Libya / Libyan .... Sudan / Sudanese ....

Morocco / Moroccan .... Tunisia / Tunisian ....

Mozambique / Mozambican .... Zimbabwe / Zimbabwean ....

Australasia

Australia / Australian .... New Zealand / New Zealander ....

The twelve most widely spoken languages

Chinese ....
English ....
Spanish ....
Hindi ....
Russian ....
Arabic ....
Portuguese ....
Japanese ....
German ....
French ....
Italian ....
Korean ....

What's the Spanish for 'Hi, there, I'm Ricky Martin's brother'?

SPANISH IN 5 DAYS

CAFÉ DE MADRID

I'm American. I'm from Los Angeles. ....

I speak English and Spanish. ....

Which languages do you speak? ....

I speak Spanish and a bit of French. ....

She's fluent in Spanish and she can get by in French. ....

I'd like to go to Peru. ....

1 Write the names of the countries and the nationalities.

Country

1 *England* ....

2 ....

3 ....

4 ....

5 ....

6 ....

7 ....

8 ....

9 ....

10 ....

Nationality

1 *English* ....

2 ....

3 ....

4 ....

5 ....

6 ....

7 ....

8 ....

9 ....

10 ....

2a Put the nationalities in exercise 1 into groups according to their spelling.

-an / -ian	-ish	-ese	Other
Italian	*English*	*Portuguese*	*Welsh*

2b Add the nationalities for these countries to exercise 2a.

Argentina	Brazil	Canada	Chile	China
Denmark	Holland	Hungary	Japan	Mexico
Poland	Sudan	Sweden	Turkey	Switzerland

3 Complete the languages.

1 J *apanese* .... is spoken in Japan.
2 I .... is spoken in Italy.
3 G .... is spoken in Germany.
4 P .... is spoken in Poland.
5 S .... is spoken in Spain.
6 E .... is spoken in New Zealand.

4 Where are these languages spoken: English, Portuguese, Spanish, French and Arabic?

Choose from the countries in the box.

Australia	Canada	France	South Africa
Chile	Portugal	Spain	Brazil
Iraq	Egypt	Argentina	Saudi Arabia

1 English is spoken in *Australia* ...., ... and ....
2 Portuguese is spoken in .... and ....
3 Spanish is spoken in ...., ... and ....
4 French is spoken in .... and ....
5 Arabic is spoken in ...., ... and ....

5 Read Ben's answers to the questionnaire, then write your own answers.

QUESTIONNAIRE

QUESTIONNAIRE QUESTIONNAIRE
QUESTIONNAIRE
QUESTIONNAIRE

Countries, nationalities and languages

1 In which country were you born?

Ben: *England* ....

You: ....

2 In which country do you live now?

Ben: *England* ....

You: ....

3 What nationality are you?

Ben: *English* ....

You: ....

4 Have you got any relatives or friends whose nationality is different from yours? Say

• who they are
• where they live
• what their nationality is
• which languages they speak

Ben: My grandmother lives in England. She's Spanish. She speaks Spanish and English. My cousins live in Spain. They're Spanish. They speak Spanish and a bit of English. My best friend at school is called Narain. He's English. His parents are from India. Narain speaks English and Hindi.

You: ....
....
....
....
....
....
....
....
....
....
....

5 Which countries have you visited?

Ben: *Spain and France* ....

You: ....

6 Which countries would you like to visit?

Ben: *I'd like to go to the USA.* ....

You: ....

7 Which languages do you speak ...
a) well? b) quite well?

a) Ben: *English (of course!)* ....
You: ....

b) Ben: *Spanish* ....
You: ....

8 In how many languages can you say *hello*? List the languages, and give the words for *hello*.

Spanish .... *¡Hola!* ....
French .... *Bonjour!* ....
....
....
....

9 Which languages are these? They all mean *thank you*.

Teşekkür ederim   ευχαριστώ

Obrigado / Obrigada

6 Answer the quiz questions.

QUIZ

How much do you know about countries, languages and nationalities?

1 With which countries do you associate these foods:

 a) pasta and pizza?

 b) fish and chips?

 c) tacos and nachos?

 d) croissants?

 e) frankfurters?

2 Which is the largest country in South America: Brazil or Chile?

....

3 Which African country is closest to Spain: Tunisia or Morocco?

....

4 In which country is the Parthenon: Greece or Egypt?

....

5 In which country is the Taj Mahal: India or Indonesia?

....

6 Which nationalities do you associate with these airlines?

ALITALIA	Greek
BA	Russian
AEROFLOT	Italian
IBERIA	Polish
OLYMPIC	German
KLM	Spanish
LUFTHANSA	Dutch
LOT	British

7 What is the name of the French-speaking province in Eastern Canada: Queensland or Quebec?

....

8 In which country do people speak German, French and Italian: Switzerland or Sweden?

....

Answers
1 a) Italy b) Britain / The UK c) Mexico d) France e) Germany 2 Brazil 3 Morocco 4 Greece 5 India
6 Alitalia Italian; BA British; Aeroflot Russian; Iberia Spanish; Olympic Greek; KLM Dutch;
Lufthansa German; LOT Polish 7 Quebec 8 Switzerland

 7 Write two quiz questions of your own. See if your friends can answer them.

 8 Write ten words and five expressions you are going to memorize.

Words	Expressions
1	1 ....
2	....
3	2 ....
4	....
5	3 ....
6	....
7	4 ....
8	....
9	5 ....
10	....

Test yourself 3 (Units 9 to 12)

How much can you remember?

1 Solve the crossword.

¹G	R	²A	P	³E	S		⁴		⁵		⁶
				⁷							
⁸					⁹						
			¹⁰								
¹¹				¹²							

Down ▼

1 A musical instrument with strings, used by rock musicians. (6)

2 People in Saudi Arabia speak this language. (6)

3 A country in North Africa, where Cleopatra was queen. (5)

4 It's a long yellow fruit. (6)

5 England, Spain, Germany and France are all countries in ... (6)

6 My grandmother never wore trousers. She always wore a skirt or a ... (5)

9 They're really fashionable ... the moment. (2)

Across ➤

1 You make wine from them. (6)

4 Have some ... and butter. (5)

7 Let's ... out for a meal. (2)

8 If you want to eat good pasta and pizza, go to ... ! (5)

9 Can I have ... orange juice, please? (2)

10 You make chips and crisps from them. (8)

11 It's good with curry. (4)

12 The USA: The United ... of America. (6)

(14 marks)

2 Your penfriend is staying with you. List seven things you can do at the weekend.

0 *We can go to a disco.* ....

1 ....

2 ....

3 ....

4 ....

5 ....

6 ....

7 ....

(6 marks)

3 Write the names of three more...

1 things you wear on a hot day   *swimming trunks* ....
2 things you wear on a cold day   *a fleece* ....
3 things you wear on your feet   *sandals* ....
4 drinks   *orange juice* ....
5 kinds of fruit   *apricot* ....
6 musical instruments   *violin* ....
7 European languages   *German* ....
8 countries in the Americas   *Venezuela* ....

(24 marks)

4 Put the words in the correct categories.

| carrot | cardigan | cauliflower | cello | coconut | celery |
| clarinet | coffee | cucumber | cheese | coat | |

food and drink	clothes	musical instruments
carrot		

(10 marks)

5 Complete the conversation.

Fay   Does this jacket .*suit*. ⁰ me?

Mum   Yes, it does. It .... ¹ really good on you.

Fay   It's a bit tight. Do you think it's too .... ²?

Mum   No, it's just right.

Fay   I don't think green suits me. Perhaps they've got it in another .... ³

Mum   They've got it in blue. Why don't you .... ⁴ the blue one on?

Fay   No, blue's boring.

Mum   And there's a red one. .... ⁵ you like that?

Fay   No, not red!

Mum   The green one's fine, Fay. How .... ⁶ is it?

Fay   £150.

Mum   Mmm. Perhaps green doesn't suit you after all.

(6 marks)

Reference

The English alphabet

Aa   Bb   Cc   Dd   Ee   Ff   Gg   Hh   Ii   Jj   Kk   Ll   Mm
Nn   Oo   Pp   Qq   Rr   Ss   Tt   Uu   Vv   Ww   Xx   Yy   Zz

Height and weight

*See Unit 3 **Describing people: age and appearance** for the use of height and weight abbreviations and symbols.*

Height	Abbreviation	Symbol	Example
ⓜ metre	m		1m
ⓜ centimetre	cm		60cm
ⓘ foot	ft	'	5ft / 5'
ⓘ inch	in	"	6in / 6"

1 metre = 3.2808 feet   1 centimetre = 0.3937 inch   1 foot = 12 inches

1m75 — one metre seventy-five   *5'9"* — five feet nine

Weight	Abbreviation	Example
ⓜ kilo	kg	3kg
ⓘ stone	st	10st
ⓘ pound	lb	8lb

1kg = 2.2046lb   14lb = 1st

64kg — sixty-four kilos   *142lb* — a hundred and forty-two pounds   *10st2lb* — ten stone two

In Britain both the metric ⓜ and imperial ⓘ systems are used. In America the imperial system is used.

Numbers

*See Unit 5 **Time** for the use of ordinal numbers in dates.*

Cardinal numbers

1 one	22 twenty-two
2 two	23 twenty-three
3 three	24 twenty-four
4 four	25 twenty-five
5 five	26 twenty-six
6 six	27 twenty-seven
7 seven	28 twenty-eight
8 eight	29 twenty-nine
9 nine	30 thirty
10 ten	40 forty
11 eleven	50 fifty
12 twelve	60 sixty
13 thirteen	70 seventy
14 fourteen	80 eighty
15 fifteen	90 ninety
16 sixteen	100 a hundred
17 seventeen	101 a hundred and one
18 eighteen	200 two hundred
19 nineteen	1,000 a thousand
20 twenty	1,000,000 a million
21 twenty-one	

Ordinal numbers

1st first	22nd twenty-second
2nd second	23rd twenty-third
3rd third	24th twenty-fourth
4th fourth	25th twenty-fifth
5th fifth	26th twenty-sixth
6th sixth	27th twenty-seventh
7th seventh	28th twenty-eighth
8th eighth	29th twenty-ninth
9th ninth	30th thirtieth
10th tenth	
11th eleventh	
12th twelfth	
13th thirteenth	
14th fourteenth	
15th fifteenth	
16th sixteenth	
17th seventeenth	
18th eighteenth	
19th nineteenth	
20th twentieth	
21st twenty-first	

Some basic spelling rules

Nouns

1 Nouns which end in -s, -ss , -sh, -ch and -x: add -es

bus	buses
address	addresses
brush	brushes
sandwich	sandwiches
box	boxes

2 Nouns which end in a consonant + o: usually, add -es

potato	potatoes
tomato	tomatoes

But if they are abbreviations, just add -s

kilo (kilogram)	kilos
photo (photograph)	photos
piano (pianoforte)	pianos
video (videocassette)	videos

3 Nouns which end in a vowel + o: add -s

radio	radios
patio	patios

4 Nouns which end in -y

-y	⟹	-ies
city		cities
country		countries
balcony		balconies
party		parties

But -y does not change after a vowel (a, e, i, o, u)

-y	⟹	-ys
boy		boys
day		days
journey		journeys

5 Nouns which end in -f(e)

-f(e)	⟹	-ves
knife		knives
leaf		leaves
wife		wives

6 Irregular plurals

child	children
foot	feet
man	men
woman	women
person	people

Verbs

1 Verbs which end in -e: drop the -e before adding -ing

come	coming
dance	dancing
hope	hoping
smile	smiling

-ie changes to -y before -ing

-ie	⟹	-y
die		dying
lie		lying

2 Verbs which end in -ss, -sh, -ch and -x: add -es to make the third person singular of the present simple

pass	passes
push	pushes
watch	watches
relax	relaxes

do and go also form the third person singular of the present tense with -es

do	does
go	goes

3 The third person singular of the present tense of *have* is irregular

have	has

4 Verbs which end in -y

-y	⟹	third person, present simple	⟹	past simple
		-ies		-ied
carry		carries		carried
try		tries		tried
tidy		tidies		tidied

-y does not change after a vowel (a, e, i, o, u)

-y	⟹	-ys	⟹	-yed
enjoy		enjoys		enjoyed
play		plays		played
buy		buys		(irregular: bought)

5 Verbs of one syllable which end in a single consonant: double the consonant before adding -ing or -ed

	-ing form	past simple
stop	stopping	stopped
plan	planning	planned
get	getting	(irregular: got)

6 When the vowel which comes before a final consonant is stressed, double the consonant to make the -ing form and the past tense

prefer	preferring	preferred

When the vowel which comes before a final consonant is not stressed, do not double the consonant

visit	visiting	visited
happen	happening	happened
remember	remembering	remembered
develop	developing	developed

 REF *See British / American spellings, 2, on page 87.*

British	American	British	American
Unit 1 *(See page 6.)*		**Unit 6** *(See page 38.)*	
Unit 2 *(See page 12.)* Mum have got	Mom have	have a shower / bath have a wash I cycle get a lift get the bus tea (as a meal) canteen	take a shower / bath wash I ride my bike get a ride take the bus – lunch room / cafeteria
Unit 3 *(See page 18.)* fair (hair) stone (in weight) well-built	light /blond (hair) – has a good build	phone someone tidy your room do the washing-up	call someone clean your room do / wash the dishes
Unit 4 *(See page 24.)* flat block (of flats) toilet	apartment apartment building bathroom / rest room (in public places)	rubbish lay the table	garbage / trash set the table
ground floor first floor (etc.) chest of drawers cupboard duvet notice board wardrobe washbasin wastepaper bin	first floor second floor (etc.) dresser / bureau closet – bulletin board closet sink wastebasket / wastepaper basket	**Unit 7** *(See page 44.)* citizenship Maths registration end-of-term exams term marks results football pitch staff room head teacher deputy head caretaker cleaner pupil choir	civics math homeroom final exams / finals semester / quarter grades scores soccer field faculty room principal vice principal head custodian custodian / janitor student chorus / choir (for church)
opposite live in … Street shop (noun) come round	across from live on … Street store come over	lessons double Art in the … team orchestra practice timetable	classes two periods of Art on the … team orchestra (rehearsal) schedule
Unit 5 *(See page 32.)* May 1st = May the first 1st May = the first of May a quarter past two ten to three autumn at the weekend	May 1st = May first – a quarter after two ten of three fall on / over the weekend	**school types** mixed school state school public school nursery (up to 5)	co-ed school public school private school pre-school (up to 5) kindergarten (4 – 5)
Monday to Friday	Monday through Friday	primary school (5 – 12)	elementary school (5 – 12)

British	American	British	American
secondary school (11 – 16 / 18) college (16 – 18) university (18+)	junior high school (12 – 14 / 15) high school (15 / 16 – 18) college (18 – 22)	**Unit 10** *(See page 64.)* trousers vest pants cardigan jumper knickers swimming trunks swimming costume trainers zip What size are you? Does it suit me?	pants / slacks undershirt underwear sweater sweater / pullover sweater panties bathing trunks / swim trunks bathing suit / swimsuit sneakers zipper What size do you wear? Does it look good on me?
Unit 8 *(See page 50.)* football American football footballer ice hockey athletics motor racing racing car match (football) sporty keen on	soccer football soccer player (ice) hockey track and field auto racing race car game (*but* boxing match) athletic interested in		
Unit 9 *(See page 58.)* free time go to the cinema film go out for a meal	spare time go to the movies movie go out to eat	**Unit 11** *(See page 70.)* aubergine courgette chips crisps milkshake (*no ice cream*) pudding yoghurt Do you fancy …?	eggplant zucchini French fries / fries potato chips milkshake (*has ice cream*) dessert yogurt Do you want …?

1 British English and American English don't only have different words; they have different spellings, too.

British English		**American English**
-our	⟹	**or**
colour		color
favourite		favorite
-re	⟹	**-er**
metre		meter
centre		center

2 In British English *l* is doubled even when the vowel before the consonant is not stressed.

travel travelling travelled

In American English, l is not doubled.

travel traveling traveling

Bye!

Self assessment and progress check

Self assessment

Fill in the chart when you have completed each unit.

	Which vocabulary sections were the most useful? (e.g. *Friendship*)	How well did you do in the exercises? very | quite | not so well Tick the correct part of the line.	You wrote down some words and expressions to memorize. How many of them can you remember? Words /10 Expressions /5	Which vocabulary sections do you need to go over again before you do the test?
1 Meeting people				
2 Family				
3 Describing people: age and appearance				
4 House and home				

Test score: / 60

5 Time				
6 Life at home				
7 School				
8 Sport				

Test score: / 60

9 Free time				
10 Fashion				
11 Food and drink				
12 Countries, languages and nationalities				

Test score: / 60

Progress check

How much of the vocabulary did you know **before** you worked through the units?
How much do you feel you know **after** working through the units?

		Less than 25%	About 50%	More than 60%
Units 1 – 4	before			
	after			
Units 5 – 8	before			
	after			
Units 9 – 12	before			
	after			